The Mini

CAT VAC

Book

Illustrated by
Sunny Eckerle

T0364013

RP Minis®
Hachette Book Group
1290 Avenue of the Americas, New York, NY 10104
www.runningpress.com
@Running_Press

First Edition: April 2022

Published by RP Minis, an imprint of Perseus Books, LLC, a
subsidiary of Hachette Book Group, Inc. The RP Minis name and
logo is a registered trademark of the Hachette Book Group.

The Hachette Speakers Bureau provides a wide range of
authors for speaking events. To find out more, go to
www.hachettespeakersbureau.com or call (866) 376-6591.

The publisher is not responsible for websites (or their content)
that are not owned by the publisher.

ISBN: 978-0-7624-7871-2

INTRODUCTION

Why do we love watching cats ride on remote vacuums? The simple answer is because it's hilarious. It's pretty entertaining watching our tiny, fierce friends interact with objects that independently move around the house much like they do. However, what if there was something more to it?

Vacuums have evolved into elite and autonomous cleaning assistants; they're basically miniature droids, programed with a mission to keep our homes dust and debris free. Once you have a remote vac bouncing around for a while, it can begin to feel like any household pet—only with far more predictable settings.

As we all know, a cat's personality can run the gamut—ranging from bold cabinet adventurer to couch potato and friendly snuggle bug to distant admirer. So, when the humble remote vacuum enters the scene, it's a true roll of the dice on how our felines will react. Will they be bold? Will they be cautious? Or will they use it to their advantage in their ongoing quest to take over the world?

What better way to celebrate this unique, lovable combo than with your very own *Desktop Cat Vac*! This miniature duo is the perfect companion for your desk or tabletop—or anywhere else you may need them! This special pair is here to remind you that life is more fun when you have someone at your side to help you out when you need it! And most importantly, that somewhere out there a cat is cruising on a vacuum, wondering how it got there.

While it's fun to explore our own archetypes, today we are going to answer the burning

question that any cat owner with
a robot vacuum wants to know . . .
What is your cat's cat vac archetype?

ANSWER THE FOLLOWING QUESTIONS TO FIND OUT!

When your cat is introduced to something new, do they . . .

A. Embrace the change and have some fun.

B. Run in the other direction.

C. Act intimidating.

D. Feel defensive, at least at first.

E. Barely pay attention; they've got their own agenda.

Select your cat's favorite thing to do.

A. Knocking things off the table
B. Running around the house at 3 am
C. Keeping a lookout for birds
D. Sleeping
E. Licking their butt

What do you think your cat's dream getaway is?

𝒜. A large garden where they can run free.

ℬ. A nice sunny spot in a beach house.

𝒞. A large loft with good pouncing spots.

𝒟. A cabin in the woods with plenty of places to scratch.

ℰ. A screened in porch with tons of toys.

What is your cat's favorite food?

A. Chicken

B. Veggies

C. Something they've caught

D. Fish

E. Whatever you are eating

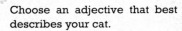

Choose an adjective that best describes your cat.

A. Loving

B. Nervous

C. Energetic

D. Distrustful

E. Unbothered

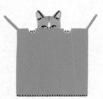

Now that you've taken the quiz, it's time to discover your cat's cat vac personality!

Mostly As—*Cruising Cat Vac*

Your cat is the *cool* cat, the one who goes with the flow. They sit proudly on the moving vehicle that appears to be built just for them. They are one with whatever life throws their way because the embody the "you've got this" attitude 100 percent. Your cat takes life by the paws and prowls the scene atop their tiny throne, enjoying the ride.

Mostly Bs—*Scaredy Cat Vac*

New things can be pretty scary when you don't know how they operate, so that makes your cat nervous or perhaps skeptical. An investigation must be performed. When something comes their way unannounced, they understandably flee in the other direction until they can make sense of it. Maybe they'll come around one day, but until some trust is built, there's no way they are going near whatever that *thing* is.

Mostly Cs—*Hunter Cat Vac*

Crouched down, ears back, laser-focused. Your cat is one with the machine! They remain on task until personal success is secured. They'll either use this contraption to their advantage and take over the world (and catch any of the mice in their way)—or stalk it until they can deliver that final, fatal pounce.

Mostly Ds—*Territorial Cat Vac*

Your cat stands their ground and doesn't take anything from anybody, especially not foreign objects that *move*! This mini vacuum wants to run into them? Wrong move, robot buddy. They'll hiss and scratch all day to defend their turf. They'll hop on, but only to throw off its sensors, propelling it into the wall. They are the only one who can occupy inconvenient places in this house.

Mostly Es—*Lazy Cat Vac*

You cat couldn't be bothered by most things; they rather just hang out and lounge and maybe throw in a couple of naps. A new toy in the house? Sure, they've seen them come and go, but lying stretched out on bags in the sunroom is your cat's favorite. Maybe they'll hop on and curl into their best ball for a chill ride. Plus, can this thing zoom them over to the kitchen for some snacks? Bonus points.

Inconclusive—*The Eclectic Cat Vac*

Your cat doesn't fit into a box (unless they want to sit in it), and why should they? There are no complex rules here! Maybe their archetype changes depending on their mood. Your cat is the sum of different parts, so their cat vac archetype should be, too!

Now that you've had some time to take the quiz and familiarize yourself with the types of cat vacs out in the wild, your *Desktop Cat Vac* would like to impart the following words of wisdom.

CAT VAC WISDOM

- 🐾 **It's okay to get stuck:** It just makes you more resourceful in developing an escape plan.

- 🐾 **Don't worry about the mess:** There's always a way to clean it up, even if it has you bumping into a few walls along the way.

🐾 **Dare to be bold:** Whether you are ready for the ride of your life or defending someone's honor, your actions matter, and so do you!

🐾 **Take time to recharge:** No one likes a grumpy cat, or worse... a dead battery!

❀ **Enjoy the ride:** Life moves faster than a cruising cat on a mini vac. It's crucial that, no matter what dust bunnies get in your way, always do your best to enjoy the ride.

No matter what kind of personality your cat may have at any given time, we can all agree that watching them interact with pretty much anything can bring a smile to our faces. We hope that this *Desktop Cat Vac* can bring that sense of joy and happiness to your desk or wherever your adventures take you and beyond!

This book has been bound using handcraft methods and Smyth-sewn to ensure durability.

The box and interior was designed by Celeste Joyce.

The text was written by Brenna Dinon.